REIGNITE THE EMBERS

E.V. NOVA

after the ashes
comes the breeze of change.
not strong, but monumental in the way it
isn't there one second,
and the next,
everything is different.
unrecognizable.
irrevocable.
and still, amid the strange puzzle of our surroundings,
we find a way to fit,
to comprehend,
and to rise.

you were just as unprepared to love me
as i was to let you go.

what's in a name?
everything.
nothing.
but it's not nothing.
today, i came across an envelope with my last name on it.
but it's not mine, is it?
not anymore.
it's yours,
and it's the final thing you took from me.
no, it's not just a name,
it was mine.
and it still hurts to see it,
scrawled on black ink and splattered tears.

i never wanted to keep you hidden like a secret,
but i wanted to keep you.
at least, until i realized
i was your dirty little secret, too.

for you, i stripped myself to bone,
covered it with the muted ensemble you wanted me to be.
for him, i stripped myself bare,
hid my pain and allowed him to awaken the flesh i thought
had died.
whether cloaked in your expectations
or opened wide by his choked promises,
i am left here, alone, in the middle of this bed,
dead unwanted skin,
a heart that doesn't want to beat,
and pain not even my tears can drown.
you don't want me.
neither does he.
and i can't blame you
because i don't want me anymore, either.

the weight of the world juggles me between feeling
like i'm too much
and not enough,
too much to handle,
not enough to love,
never the right amount of anything to matter.

you had an answer for everything,
even though your lies became so tangled that you couldn't
remember which one commenced your downward spiral.
you always knew what to say,
and believed in the flimsy justification you offered for your
betrayals.
you had answers, and beliefs, and you had words as
weapons,
but there's one thing you forgot while building the fortress of
your renewed existence with tarnished brass mistaken for
gold,
while sputtering prison sentences disguised as fairy tales,
while you were waiting cowardly in the corner for me to go...
you forgot to ask me to stay.
funny how your memory has returned
now that your misguided fortress has started to corrode in the
steadying breaths of oxygen i've begun to inhale without you.

i don't mourn the loss of you,
i mourn the loss of me,
the one who believed and trusted and understood the good in
the world.
i don't miss you,
i miss me,
the girl with the heart on her sleeve,
willing to love all your faults and phantoms and imperfec-
tions like they were my own.
i am over you,
but not the way you treated me,
unabashed neglect and cruelty for the sake of your own sins.
no, i'm not past the pain,
and the pain may never truly pass,
but i will keep putting one foot in front of the other,
toward my chance at healing from the scars you left,
and away from the shackles of my own insecurities that you
used to tie me down without so much as a single touch.

there's being alone,
and there's being lonely.
one is peaceful solitude.
the other is you.

i believed you were the one.
but you weren't.
i was wrong.
i was the one…
the one who believed in you
when you didn't believe in us.
the one who made vows and meant them
while you broke them, broke me.
the one who embraced your last name,
just for you to take it away.
the one who waited for you to choose me
when instead you chose the idea of her.
i'm also the one who picked up your shirts,
and picked up the pieces.
the one who feared life without you,
yet let new life find me instead.
the one who lived to be yours
and now lives to be me.
with each day, i'm finding out who i really am,
all because you weren't the one.

it didn't kill me,
but it didn't make me stronger, either.
it made me different,
forever changed,
harder in some ways, softer in others.
but in the end, I'm not stronger.
i was always strong.
even in the moments of weakness.
standing here, wavering on the other side of that hell, isn't
merely proof,
it's the truth...of that strength.
of my strength.
and i paid dearly to own it.

if you can trade our forever
for her potential,
then i can trade my shattered heart
for a new beginning,
a chance to give its broken pieces to someone
who does not fear being cut by them.

my memories are of him.
my fantasies are of you.
but my now is me, only me,
because he left me behind,
and you haven't found me yet.

you shine in the shadows
brighten despite being eclipsed
smile despite the savagery
whisper despite the screams that strangle you
stay despite every reason to leave.

i could let you whisper your promises,
reach for me,
press my hands beneath your palms,
kiss my neck, my mouth, my soul,
take me apart with your fingertips,
put me back together with your mind,
and still, you would not own me.

she can look you in the eye and feel the passionate heat of
your stare,
but if your actions are rooted in now,
not always,
she'll leave you there.

you're a ghost but you linger
in the words you whispered across my skin,
in the gasps still trapped in tepid air,
in the scent of sweat and spice still infused in cotton sheets,
in the dark shadows of your gaze still burned in my retinas,
in the taste of you still coating my tongue.
you're a ghost, long gone,
but you're still here.

you asked me questions last night,
prodded at the passion that both unsettles me and makes me
whole,
accepted the flaws i revealed and sent subtle signals of
sincerity.
the answers to those questions, while important,
mean nothing compared to the simple fact that you cared
enough to ask at all.

your broad shoulders eclipse my fragile form
just as they block out the sun.
the thickness of your arms could crush me if you decided to,
but could also cradle my frayed frame if i let you.
what you decide and what i allow determine where we go
next,
whether i'll hand you the kryptonite to destroy what little of
me remains,
or entwine your harbored strength in mine, becoming
stronger than the storm that brought me to my knees,
then guided me to crawl toward you.

the flavor of your eyes shining in the moonlight as you pull
me against your skin
is the taste i crave with the hunger of a woman starved.
it makes no sense, yet i know it with every cell in my body.

you are a raw wound,
a tangled web of fantasy,
a taste of reckless devotion,
a beautiful addiction,
an untamed love,
an unspoken necessity.

i don't blame you for the tingle across my skin
or the damp thoughts that seep from my mind to my most
sensitive flesh,
even though i know you're the reason for both,
cause and effect,
fire and gasoline,
and you could ease my trembling desire with the slightest
touch of your fingers in places we don't speak of, only feel,
explore,
possess,
claim as your own.

you can want her body
like any boy does,
but it's her mind that will set you ablaze
and make you a man.

you want to permeate my body,
drink in my essence,
taste the elixir of my desire,
but i won't allow you
the privilege
until every nerve ending and synapse and fiber of your being
is screaming as it falls over the precipice of wanting
into the dark, moonlit valley of desperate need.

just breathe.
let your shoulders lower,
feel your heart race.
there is a moment when someone reaches inside you
and you submit to the way their fingers caress your soul,
a moment when there's no turning back because their touch
has left impressions on the deepest parts of you.
this is ours.

there's a war raging inside me as while I don't trust your
heart,
i believe every tingle and shiver of your body as it comes
alive beneath my fingertips.

the water scalds my skin
and the whiskey sears my throat,
but nothing compares to the burn of your touch
or the raging fire you ignite in my soul.

if i thought
for a moment
i could use you
to tame me,
i would let you loose,
free to run wild
among my curves and contours,
using me to set you free, too.
but i can't,
i won't,
because i don't believe
there is a way
that losing ourselves in each other
would ever be enough
to tame the venom in your blood
or mine
that keeps us poisoned
by the needs that course through us,
a fever that will never break.

i love that my mouth
can bring you to your knees,
not by uttering words,
but by evoking your darkest desires,
your deepest needs,
and letting them dance on the tip of my tongue.

take me as i am,
and you can take me as you want.

a fiery touch
a desperate whimper
entwined fingers
a gasp of breath
flesh on flesh
fingertips robbing lungs of air
but giving the most intense pleasure.
trembling hands
and quivering limbs
the taste of desire
the moan of need
rising, building, a hopeless fiery crash.
this is us.

your eyes alone can dampen my flesh and ignite my
thoughts.
your voice can command in a whisper.
but it's your touch, gentle and raw and sure,
that can elicit the most desperate pleas
and force me to my knees,
unapologetically begging for whatever remnants of affection
you'll give.

if i told you that your touch affected me so deeply i thought
i'd die,
would you touch me again and make me feel alive?

hold me down,
pin me beneath you,
press your fingers to my throat,
overpower me,
keep me captive,
set me free.

if you knew all the things
i've done to you in my thoughts,
the way our bodies come alive beneath each other's fingertips,
the way my desire would taste on your tongue,
the way your control would suffer but your heart would soar,
you'd be here, right now,
wearing that knowing grin
and barely contained fire in your eyes.

i want to guide you down the stairs,
between the pristine sheets of my bed,
and remind you what it's like
to touch the soul of the sky,
make its back arch in blissful agony,
and elicit lightning from its deepest depths among the stars.

you are so much, too much,
and yet i can never get enough.
still, i fear you.
i shy away.
i'm not ready to be loved
with your brand of crazy and passion.
but i hope to.
i want to.
someday.
i pray you do, too,
when the stone of your walls crumbles,
when the armored threads of distrust finally fray,
you'll not just fuck me, but feel me.
and i'll feel you, too.
feel loved,
feel right.
and we'll make it, unapologetically,
someday.

it's not that we don't want to be alone.
it's that we don't want to be lonely in someone else's presence.
choose me,
include me,
remind me that we're 'us' in this crazy world,
and we'll never know lonely again.

fingertips reveal weakness,
promises reveal temptation,
gasps reveal desperation,
ripped lace reveals bare flesh,
brown eyes reveal fire,
dampness reveals desire,
your name in the dark reveals my undoing.

the words on the screen emit your smile.
the spaces between the words
hold unspoken promises.
the syllables i sound out
taste like sugary acceptance
and spiced anticipation.
each letter you type to me
pushes me closer to the edge where the rock crumbles.
if i fall,
you're going down with me.
because i will not jump,
i will not free fall willingly.
if i careen from the precipice,
it will be because you pushed me.
you'll have no one to blame but yourself.
and i will blame you, too.

you kiss a trail down my neck
as i graze my nails up your back.
you thrust every inch of your desire inside me,
invading me, beneath you,
as i arch up to meet your hunger with my own unsatiated
need.
we collide,
we mesh,
moving as one.
but we are not one.
we're us.
combined.
entangled.
twisted together in our own knotted cocoon of sweet clandes-
tine chaos.
no, we are not one.
but together, we're everything.

during the day i revisit the night
if only to feel the intoxicating pressure of your fingers
around my throat
and the intense release awakened within me
as i succumb to you completely.

our love is a bomb,
so much,
too much.
pressure building,
constricting me,
undoing you,
threatening our strength,
our foundation,
trembling with each tick as the clock counts down
to the moment time ends,
when we become nothing,
become everything,
and we burst in a blinding kaleidoscopic blast,
left in pieces of who we were,
what we became,
and what remains in the wake of our beautiful disaster.

there is no star in the midnight sky that burns as brightly
as your eyes
when your desire overflows
and attempts to drown me in its glittery blaze.

the pressure,
the pulsing,
the pounding.
we are poison in each other's veins,
pooling at the base of our hearts,
arrhythmic, erratic,
fatal.

the abstract masterpiece of reddened streaks down your back
is an artistic,
raw reminder of the way you drive me to painful pleasure
that wreaks havoc
on my control and sets my sensual creativity alight.

i'd pop the sweet drug on my tongue
and swallow
if i thought it would curb
the intoxication of you
burning through my bloodstream,
but i don't,
there's no use,
because there is no high i can chase
that will rival what you do to my mind,
my body,
my control,
my heart.

beads of sweat on skin
dampness from within
slow and steady, you stir something inside me,
awakening the devil who desires you,
daring me to dance in your shadow,
to straddle the boundary of love and lust,
to unveil myself to you,
to do the unimaginable – to trust.

my eyes struggle to adjust to your brand of darkened desire,
as does my body,
but if you're patient,
if your rough hands hold me secure, not as a slave but as
sinful royalty beneath your fingertips,
i'll give myself to you and do anything you'd ever want,
held captive by the seduction in your stare
and the safety of your soul.

my eyes squeeze shut
as i savor the intensity of you,
so deep,
so intoxicating,
the way we pulse together,
our instinctive need for each other smothering our fears,
fanning the embers of our hope,
unearthing trust in the wasteland of our tainted minds.
nothing matters—our thoughts, our doubts, our pasts or
scars.
there's only us,
only the way you feel inside me,
only the way you calm me and ignite me
simultaneously,
only the way we lose ourselves in the peaceful chaos we've
found.
your gaze penetrates mine
as you push deeper,
as i gasp your name,
as i fall.
it may be your name on my tongue,
mixed with the salt of your skin and the spicy sweetness of
our kiss,
but it's more than that--
a confession,
a truth i can no longer lie to myself about.
you are my biggest fear,
my greatest hope,
my deepest desire,
and through my eyes, still squeezed shut in undeniable
ecstasy,
there's no way for me to see the naked beauty in your choco-
late eyes,

no reason for me to feel more than the bliss you've set alight
within my body,
but i do.
i see it all.
and i believe it. believe you.
and with another deep stroke,
you remind me to believe me, too.

the darkness we hide in
masks the darkness we are.
yet, nothing can protect us from the bright explosion that cuts
through the night when we share the shadows,
when we own our darkest desires,
when we take what is ours,
and set ourselves free.

come to me
in the peace and quiet.
bring your chaos,
and i will pierce the silence
with the desperate sound of your name.
touch me
in the places no one else sees.
leave marks on my skin,
and we'll reminisce about the road map of your desire
i so proudly wear.
kiss my mouth
and taste how much i need you.
invade me as we both slip slowly beneath the rising tide,
where i drown in the desperate truth of how much you need
me, too.

trusting you, after him, is hard.
but losing you, after us, would be worse.
we can't go back,
pretend you didn't change everything,
pretend you didn't make me believe.
make me love.
make me whole.

i anticipate your words when you're away
the way i anticipate your touch when you're here.
i long for your voice to tangle with my mind
the way i long for the taste of you
to linger on my lips.
i get lost in your fantasies
the way i lose myself as you become one of mine.
you don't need to leave a lazy trail of fingerprints on my skin
to touch me.
we needn't be in the same room, desperate for the same air as
our limbs entwine and our hearts become frenzied birds in
their golden cages.
you needn't touch me,
yet, touch me you do.

my lungs
will run out
of breath
long before
my body
ever tires
of your touch

if you keep your voice and your roaming fingertips out of my
sweet dreams tonight,
i will finally get some sleep.
but be damned if that rest will be worth it,
knowing i was deprived of you to get it.

i hear you like you're here,
but i long for you because you're there.
i taste your memory,
and i crave your touch,
even though i feel you everywhere.

the clock ticks so loudly,
counting down each second
until the moment time stops,
our eyes lock,
and i'm lost in your love once again.

slip beneath the cotton sheets
and devour me like a main course,
beginning with only sweet nibbles
as your hunger overtakes your restraint
and you slowly lose control,
consuming me until i'm finished,
only bare bones on a silver plate,
your desire picked clean until you reach for me once more,
unsatiated, never fully satisfied,
always ready for your next meal.

can you taste the memory of me on your mouth?
can you feel the pulse of my need electrifying the air you
breathe?
do my gasps for breath still infiltrate your mind and clutch at
your most sinful thoughts?
am i your dirtiest secret, or your wildest fantasy?
does your skin still carry traces of me?
of who we are?
of what we could be?
do these questions blaze in your eyes as you drink in my
submission?
do they destroy you with their hidden reckless beauty?
tell me, do i?

your breath whispers across my skin
like a dandelion petal in the breeze,
making a wish,
making *me* wish,
you'd do it again,
forever.

i don't need
a ticket to paradise
to find bliss.
i've already found it
in the safety of your arms
and the promise of your kiss.

i have spent
so much time
believing my love
is too much,
that i am not enough,
that i need to be hidden away
among the shadows,
a dark little secret,
an ebony smudge on my pristine angel wings,
when the reality is
my love is so potent,
the right one will never find enough ways
to make my body sing
and my heart take flight,
but he'll spend the rest of my life
trying.

i do not need your arms around me,
but i want them.
want you.
because while i could exist without you,
i could never truly live,
and i'd be a shell of the woman
i become beneath your fingertips

i love that you know i sometimes like it rough.
i adore that you know i sometimes need it gentle.
but i'm in love with the fact that no words are required for
you to know which i crave, and when.

something happened
along the way
you became more than
somewhere you rest
while i licked my wounds
you became the balm
that covered my ragged edges
and soothed my fractured mind
while your gentle touch healed the scars on my skin
and your heart hummed a coaxing lullaby i'd thought
i'd long since forgotten.

i cling to your words in your absence
the way i wrap myself in your body when you're here,
allow each of them to be buried deep inside me,
penetrate me,
cause my soul to cry out in feverish bliss,
because while your words are merely spoken, they touch me,
tear at my skin and bruise my lips,
they own me,
just as you will, then.
just as you do, always.

all my dreams are coming true,
the ones i've dreamed for as long as i can remember,
and the ones i didn't know i had until i met you.

it's becoming clearer
as the days go by
why my wounds had to open,
why my heart had to die,
why the war had to rage
so viciously inside,
and why i had to shed my skin to become the me i'm meant
to be.

i'm not perfect,
and that's okay.
i'm not okay,
and that's normal.
i'm not normal,
but no one is.
and I'm not 'no one.'
i'm me.
and that's perfectly, crazily, unapologetically okay.

the saying goes,
'i wish I'd met you sooner so i could love you longer.'
but that's not true.
because if i'd met you sooner,
i don't believe i would have appreciated you,
and you wouldn't have appreciated me.
you wouldn't have been through your hell,
and i wouldn't have weathered the storm that threatened to
bury me,
but we wouldn't have recognized the hurt in each other's
eyes,
wouldn't have understood the scars we wear like mute birds
on our shoulders,
watching and wary,
saying nothing but scrutinizing everything, whether it's real
or not.
we wouldn't be the same people who fought so hard to trust
and won.
so, i don't wish i'd met you sooner,
i only wish for one thing:
to love you, unconditionally, imperfectly,
and with everything i truly am, now, in this late but very real
moment,
and to have you wish the same.

if i told you i love you,
would you confess the same?
or would you continue to keep it hidden
in the drunken stares you offer me sober,
in the gentleness of your fingertips on the small of my back,
in the texts and calls i didn't ask for but adore,
in the stirring of my coffee as you make it just the way i
like it,
in the thank yous and gratitude and playfulness we speak of,
safely, instead?

you ask me what love is to me.
it is you.
it is us.
it is the imperfections we wear like diamonds
and the softness of our savage hearts.
it is the way we hold each other together,
even from a distance,
and know irrevocably that no touch or whisper or promise of
forever
will ever be enough.
yet, we are.
enough.
together, we irrevocably are.

you don't make me whole.
don't mistake that for some unwitting bravery on my part, or
the idea that you aren't intertwined in my happiness.
you don't make me whole,
but you let me be me.
just me.
all me.
unwavering and undeniable.
me.
and it's me who is whole.
me.
the one you let me be with you,
the one you don't try to change.
and i'll thank you–and love you–for that, forever.

i find simplicity with you among the chaos,
sunshine throughout the storm,
challenge among the acceptance,
and beauty amidst the scars.
it makes no sense,
yet what i've found with you i adore and understand
with crystal clarity.

i sit at the kitchen table
of my little house
aware of the bare walls
and silent rooms.
but it's okay.
i feel no desire to cover these walls,
or create sound in the silence,
because i met you,
and this is not home.
you are.

a year ago, i didn't know you,
didn't remember you,
didn't love you.
i didn't know the taste of your kiss,
the sound of your name on my tongue,
the sound of mine on yours,
or the feel of your touch in the dark.
i didn't wait for you to come home,
didn't know about your past,
didn't know about our future.
no, i didn't wait for you,
but i'd been waiting all along.
i just didn't know it yet.

a year can change everything.
a year ago tonight,
i lie in bed, wondering what was wrong.
a year ago tomorrow,
i sat there between rumpled sheets as you sliced my heart out
with a few sharpened words.
a year later, you're a memory,
a 'used to be,'
a 'left behind,'
because i'm a memory, too.
a year later,
i'm a different person.
a year later,
i don't wonder what's wrong,
i don't wonder where i stand,
and i don't wonder who i am.
a year later,
i am me.
and me without you is someone i can't wait to take on the
next year with.

betrayal does not kill us,
though it ends us,
just the same.
who we were,
what we thought we wanted,
is no more.
but the embers of our true selves never die,
always smoldering amid strangled smoke,
waiting for a reason
to come alight,
and reignite,
again.

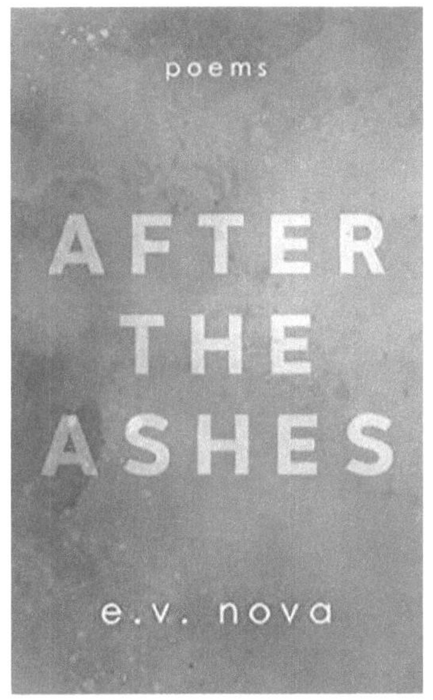
poems
AFTER
THE
ASHES
e.v. nova

ABOUT THE AUTHOR

E.V. Nova is a Canadian author and poet with a love for raw, devastatingly beautiful words. She believes in the power of turning pain into poetry, just as much as she believes everything happens for a reason.

Connect with E.V. Nova on Instagram and Facebook @evnovaofficial.

ABOUT THE PUBLISHER

Harbor Lane Books, LLC is a US-based independent, digital publisher of commercial fiction, non-fiction, and poetry.

Connect with Harbor Lane Books on their website www.harborlanebooks.com and TikTok, Instagram, Facebook, Twitter, and Pinterest @harborlanebooks.